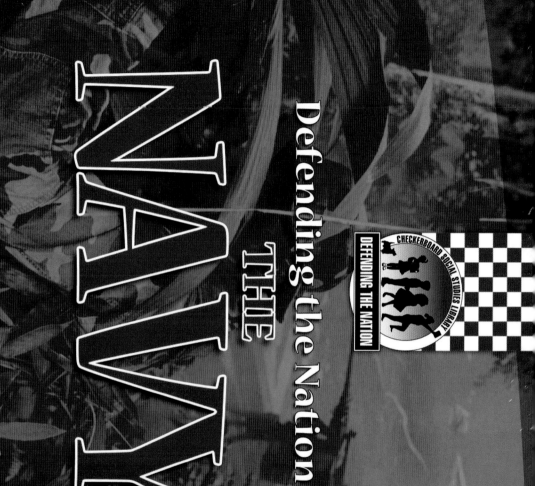

Defending the Nation

THE
NAVY

John Hamilton

ABDO Publishing Company

DEFENDING THE NATION

CHECKERBOARD SOCIAL STUDIES LIBRARY

visit us at
www.abdopublishing.com

Published by ABDO Publishing Company, 4940 Viking Drive, Edina, Minnesota 55435.
Copyright © 2007 by Abdo Consulting Group, Inc. International copyrights reserved in all countries. No part of this book may be reproduced in any form without written permission from the publisher. The Checkerboard Library™ is a trademark and logo of ABDO Publishing Company.

Printed in the United States.

Cover Photos: front, U.S. Navy; back, U.S. Air Force
Interior Photos: Corbis pp. 1, 12, 13, 21; Getty Images pp. 5, 11; North Wind pp. 8-9; U.S. Air Force p. 15; U.S. Navy pp. 5, 10, 16-17, 19, 20, 23, 24, 25, 27, 28-29

Series Coordinator: Megan M. Gunderson
Editors: Rochelle Baltzer, Megan M. Gunderson
Art Direction & Cover Design: Neil Klinepier

Library of Congress Cataloging-in-Publication Data

Hamilton, John, 1959-
   The Navy / John Hamilton.
      p. cm. -- (Defending the nation)
   Includes index.
   ISBN-13: 978-1-59679-760-4
   ISBN-10: 1-59679-760-6
   1. United States. Navy--Juvenile literature. I. Title II. Series: Hamilton, John, 1959- .
Defending the nation.

VA58.4.H26 2006
359.00973--dc22
                                                    2005028754

Contents

The U.S. Navy

The U.S. military exists to protect America and its people. The military is trained to defeat America's enemies. It is equally ready to help prevent war. And, it assists people during natural disasters. When hurricanes or earthquakes strike, the U.S. military is often there to help.

The U.S. Navy is a big part of the U.S. military. It is the largest and most powerful navy on Earth. The navy helps protect America from invasion. It also helps keep the oceans safe for shipping. The U.S. Navy can fight wars almost anywhere in the world. To carry out its missions, the navy uses a combination of surface ships, aircraft, and submarines.

It is the navy's job to help preserve peace and security in the United States. The men and women of today's U.S. Navy are volunteers. They freely give their time, and sometimes their lives, to defend their country.

Sailors man the rails as the USS Bonhomme Richard leaves port.

The U.S. Navy flag is not flown on each ship. Instead, it is used for ceremonies.

Timeline

1775 - On October 13, the Continental Congress established the Continental navy.

1784 - The Continental navy was disbanded.

1798 - On April 30, Congress established the Department of the Navy.

1845 - The U.S. Naval Academy in Annapolis, Maryland, was established on October 10.

1862 - In April, Admiral David Farragut led the capture of the port of New Orleans, Louisiana, during the American Civil War.

1910 - Eugene Ely became the first person to fly an airplane off a U.S. cruiser.

1915 - On March 3, the Navy Reserve was established.

1941 - On December 7, Japanese armed forces attacked the Pearl Harbor naval base on Oahu, Hawaii.

1954 - The first nuclear-powered submarine was built.

1961 - The first nuclear-powered aircraft carrier was built.

1976 - The U.S. Naval Academy began accepting women midshipmen.

- The "USS" before a navy ship's name stands for "United States Ship." Other countries use similar abbreviations. In Great Britain, navy ships have "HMS" before their names. This can mean "Her Majesty's Ship" or "His Majesty's Ship."

- The tomb of Revolutionary War hero John Paul Jones is at the U.S. Naval Academy in Annapolis, Maryland. There, midshipmen guard the tomb 24 hours a day, 365 days a year.

- The Core Values of the Navy are "honor, courage, and commitment."

- Women go through the same kinds of training as men. But, there are two kinds of jobs women are not allowed to have. Women cannot serve on submarines. And, they may not join the Navy SEALs. SEALs are the navy's special forces troops.

History of the Navy

The United States of America began as a group of 13 individual British colonies. The colonies fought for their independence from Great Britain during the **Revolutionary War.** During the war, the **Continental Congress** led the colonies.

On June 14, 1775, Congress formed the Continental army to fight the British. Congress needed ships to help supply this army. So, it established the Continental navy on October 13, 1775. In total, more than 50 ships served in the Continental navy during the war.

Each navy ship had a specific job. Some defended America's ports and coastlines. Others delivered supplies to American forces. And, still others fought the British at sea.

In 1784, the Continental navy was **disbanded** because the war had ended. But U.S. cargo ships quickly became easy prey for pirates. This made the government realize how important a navy was to the country's defense, even in peacetime. So, it ordered six new ships under the Naval Act of March 1794. Then on April 30, 1798, the U.S. Congress created the Department of the Navy and further expanded the **fleet**.

The Alliance was part of the Continental navy.

The USS Constitution is the oldest commissioned navy boat that is still on the water. Visitors can see it at its home in Boston, Massachusetts.

The navy has fought in many wars during its long history. In the **War of 1812**, America's tiny **fleet** of ships fought a much larger British force. Still, the USS *Constitution* won many battles. While fighting the HMS *Guerrière*, British shot bounced off the *Constitution's* sturdy oak hull. This earned the ship its nickname, Old Ironsides. Even today, it is still officially part of the navy.

Over the years, new technology continued to help the U.S. Navy advance. Strong ships made of steel and powered by steam were built after the American **Civil War**. And in 1910, Eugene Ely became the first person to fly an airplane off a U.S. cruiser. The following year, he both landed on and took off from the battleship *Pennsylvania.* Today, the navy depends on this cooperation between air and sea forces.

By **World War II**, the navy included submarines and aircraft carriers. These greatly increased America's naval power. But on December 7, 1941, Japanese armed forces tested that strength. They conducted a sneak attack on the U.S. naval base at Pearl Harbor on Oahu, Hawaii. Despite heavy American losses, the Japanese forces failed to cripple the U.S. Navy.

The modern navy also includes **nuclear**-powered ships and submarines. The first nuclear-powered submarine was built in 1954. And in 1961, the first nuclear-powered aircraft carrier was built. All these advances mean that today, the U.S. Navy rules the waves.

Today, a memorial to those lost in the Pearl Harbor attack sits over the sunken USS Arizona.

Great Navy Commanders

Brave sailors have led the U.S. Navy throughout its history.

During the **Revolutionary War**, Captain John Paul Jones became the first well-known hero of the navy. Jones was born in Scotland in 1747 and learned to sail aboard English merchant ships. In 1775, he joined the Continental navy. And in 1779, he commanded the *Bonhomme Richard.*

In September of that year, the *Bonhomme Richard* fought Great Britain's HMS *Serapis.* At first, the battle went poorly for Jones's crew. So, the British commander asked Jones if he wanted to surrender. Hearing this, Jones yelled, "I have not yet begun to fight!" The Americans eventually won the battle, and Jones's phrase became famous.

Admiral David Farragut bravely served during the American **Civil War.** Farragut's

Captain John Paul Jones

Today, there are ships named after some of the navy's greatest commanders. And, there is a new USS Bonhomme Richard (above).

bold actions in April 1862 led to the capture of the port of New Orleans, Louisiana. This victory was very important. It blocked a major supply route for the Confederate forces. In 1864, Farragut also won a great victory in the battle of Mobile Bay. He was promoted to admiral in 1866.

Admiral Hyman G. Rickover is known as the "father of the atomic submarine." After serving in the Navy Department's Bureau of Ships during **World War II**, he studied **nuclear** energy. He led the navy's effort to use nuclear power to run many of its ships and submarines.

Organization

The U.S. military, including the navy, is organized by a hierarchy. That means there are many levels of authority. In the navy, there are both officers and **enlisted** sailors. The highest-ranking officers are admirals. They make very big decisions.

The head of the military is the president of the United States. He or she is called the commander in chief. The **Founding Fathers** wanted to be sure that the military didn't have too much power. That is one reason the head of the U.S. armed forces is the president. The president is a **civilian**, and an elected official, rather than a member of the military.

The president appoints a civilian as the secretary of the navy. The secretary heads the Department of the Navy. A military leader, the chief of naval operations, serves on the Joint Chiefs of Staff. This person advises both the secretary of the navy and the president.

Ranks

There are many ranks for sailors in the U.S. Navy. A rank is a level of responsibility. Sailors can move up in rank by showing leadership and loyalty, by length of service, or by passing special exams.

Officer Ranks

Ensign (O-1)

Lieutenant Junior Grade (O-2)

Lieutenant (O-3)

Lieutenant Commander (O-4)

Commander (O-5)

Captain (O-6)

Rear Admiral Lower Half (O-7)

Rear Admiral Upper Half (O-8)

Vice Admiral (O-9)

Admiral (O-10)

Fleet Admiral (Wartime only)

O-1

O-5

O-10

The letter and number next to each rank indicates a person's pay grade.

Warrant Officer Ranks

Warrant Officer 1 (W-1)

Chief Warrant Officer 2 (W-2)

Chief Warrant Officer 3 (W-3)

Chief Warrant Officer 4 (W-4)

Chief Warrant Officer (W-5)

W-1

W-2

W-3

W-4

Enlisted Ranks

Seaman Recruit (E-1)

Seaman Apprentice (E-2)

Seaman (E-3)

Petty Officer Third Class (E-4)

Petty Officer Second Class (E-5)

Petty Officer First Class (E-6)

Chief Petty Officer (E-7)

Senior Chief Petty Officer (E-8)

Master Chief Petty Officer (E-9)

Fleet Command Master Chief Petty Officer (E-9)

Master Chief Petty Officer of the Navy (E-9)

E-3

E-6

E-9

E-4

E-9

Today, there are about 500,000 people serving in the U.S. Navy. About 300,000 are **enlisted**, active-duty sailors. Another 52,000 are active-duty officers. And, more than 130,000 serve in the reserve forces. Reservists are trained sailors who are only called to action when the navy needs additional assistance.

In today's navy, every job requires special skills. Enlistees receive training in a specific field. They may be assigned directly to a ship for on-the-job training. Officers are specially trained in leadership skills. They give orders to enlisted sailors and other officers who are lower in rank.

Most people serving in the navy work on ships or on naval bases. Ships work together in **fleets**. Fleets are assigned to certain areas of the world. For example, the Fifth Fleet patrols the waters of the Middle East.

Naval bases are located in the United States and in many countries friendly to the United States. Some bases have airstrips so that navy airplanes can take off and land. Naval bases with shipyards can build and repair ships. The navy also operates supply centers, which have fuel, food, weapons, and ammunition.

Some navy ships travel up the Elizabeth River to Norfolk Naval Shipyard in Virginia for repairs.

Training

A person must be between 17 and 34 years old to join the U.S. Navy. Only U.S. citizens or legal **immigrants** may join. The navy prefers **enlistees** who have already graduated from high school. Officers need even more education. A college degree is usually required.

Future sailors take either the oath of enlistment or the oath of office when joining the navy. They must promise to "support and defend the Constitution of the United States against all enemies." Then, they are on their way to becoming sailors in the U.S. Navy.

When enlistees join the navy, they agree to a service commitment. This means they promise to serve in the navy for a certain number of years after their training. The length of service is generally four to six years.

New enlistees, or recruits, must complete a strict training program. Basic training, or boot camp, lasts for nine weeks. During this time, recruits become physically fit and learn how to take orders. They also learn how to use weapons, such as M16 rifles and 12-gauge shotguns. When their training is complete, recruits officially graduate as sailors in the U.S. Navy. Soon, they receive advanced training. Sailors can learn a wide variety of skills to use in their navy careers. Advanced training fields include **aviation**, electronics, engineering, world languages, and computers.

After training, sailors begin their tour of duty on a ship or on a naval base. Sailors move up in rank depending on length of service. They also take tests to qualify for promotions. The highest rank for an **enlisted** sailor is master chief petty officer of the navy.

Recruits taking the oath of enlistment

Navy officers receive different training than **enlisted** members. Many future officers train at the U.S. Naval Academy in Annapolis, Maryland. The navy began training officers there on October 10, 1845. Women were admitted for the first time in 1976.

Officers in training, or midshipmen, receive a college degree after four years of study at the academy. Naval academy graduates are required to serve five years of active duty in the navy. This is because the government pays for their education.

People who already have a college degree may begin at the 13-week Officer Candidate School. There, they

A midshipman at the U.S. Naval Academy

study naval warfare and history. Officer candidates also study subjects such as mathematics and science. And, they participate in physical training. But most important, all future officers learn leadership skills.

Officers are separated into four categories, including line, staff, limited duty, and warrant officer. Line officers might manage a naval base or work as an engineer. Staff officers are often doctors or lawyers. Limited-duty and warrant officers are **enlisted** sailors who have become officers. They usually work in administrative roles or have a technical specialty.

Midshipmen focus on both academics and physical fitness at the U.S. Naval Academy.

Navy Reserve

The Navy Reserve provides support to the U.S. Navy whenever and wherever needed. After **enlisting**, reservists go through an initial 17-day training program. Then, they train one weekend each month. They also attend annual training for two weeks each year. So, they are always ready for service.

The history of the Navy Reserve is as long as that of the U.S. Navy. It was officially established on March 3, 1915. But reserve sailors have been serving the United States in times of war since the **Revolutionary War**. During the **Persian Gulf War**, more than 21,000 navy reservists were called to duty. Today, reserve sailors are helping fight **terrorism** across the world.

The Navy Reserve is organized in the same hierarchy as the regular navy. Enlisted sailors start as seaman recruits. Officers start as ensigns and can work their way up to the rank of admiral. The Navy Reserve represents 20 percent of U.S. naval forces. It is a vital part of the U.S. Navy's success.

Some sailors enter the Navy Reserve through the Naval Reserve Officers' Training Corps (ROTC). The Naval ROTC program operates in colleges across the nation. Naval ROTC students are called midshipmen. Midshipmen add naval science courses to their regular class load. After graduation, they become ensigns and are required to serve in the navy for three to eight years.

Navy reservists specialize in certain fields just like active-duty sailors.

Warships and Aircraft

The U.S. Navy uses many different kinds of surface ships. Some are small tugboats that hold only a few sailors. Others are huge and hold thousands. Aircraft carriers such as the USS *Theodore Roosevelt* can carry almost 6,000 people and 85 aircraft. The *Theodore Roosevelt* is 1,092 feet (333 m) long.

Today's navy uses task forces, which are groups of ships that travel together. Usually, a task force includes at least one aircraft carrier. In addition, it has smaller ships with special weapons and strengths.

Aircraft such as the F-14D Tomcat can launch directly from the flight deck of the USS Theodore Roosevelt.

Task forces are also supported by supply ships. These carry food, fuel, and ammunition. Destroyers and cruisers work together to protect the task force against enemy ships, airplanes, and submarines.

The role of large battleships changed after **World War II**. Instead of fighting major battles at sea, the navy began helping forces on land. So today, the navy mainly relies on aircraft and missiles to fight wars. Modern **cruise missiles** can hit targets more than 1,500 miles (2,400 km) away.

The navy uses many kinds of airplanes. These include the F-14 Tomcat, the F/A-18 Hornet, the EA-6B Prowler, the S-3B Viking, and the E-2 Hawkeye. Naval aircraft fly many kinds of missions, including searching for enemy ships and submarines. And, some navy airplanes can take off from aircraft carriers.

With new Tomahawk Block IV cruise missiles, the navy will be able to change a cruise missile's target after it is launched.

Submarines

Today, submarines are among the most feared weapons the navy uses. They are very difficult for an enemy to find. And, they can hide at great depths in the ocean for months at a time! The U.S. Navy is the best in the world in undersea warfare. Its **fleet** of submarines is very powerful.

Attack submarines seek out and destroy both enemy submarines and surface ships. They are quiet and fast. And, they are well armed with powerful torpedoes and **cruise missiles**. The U.S. Navy has nearly 60 attack submarines in its fleet. One is the USS *Seawolf*. It is 353 feet (108 m) long and holds a crew of 140.

Ballistic missile submarines are bigger than attack submarines. The USS *Nevada* is 560 feet (171 m) long, with a crew of 155. It can fire powerful Trident ballistic missiles. There are 18 ballistic missile submarines in the U.S. fleet.

The U.S. Navy also uses submarines such as the USS Dolphin for research.

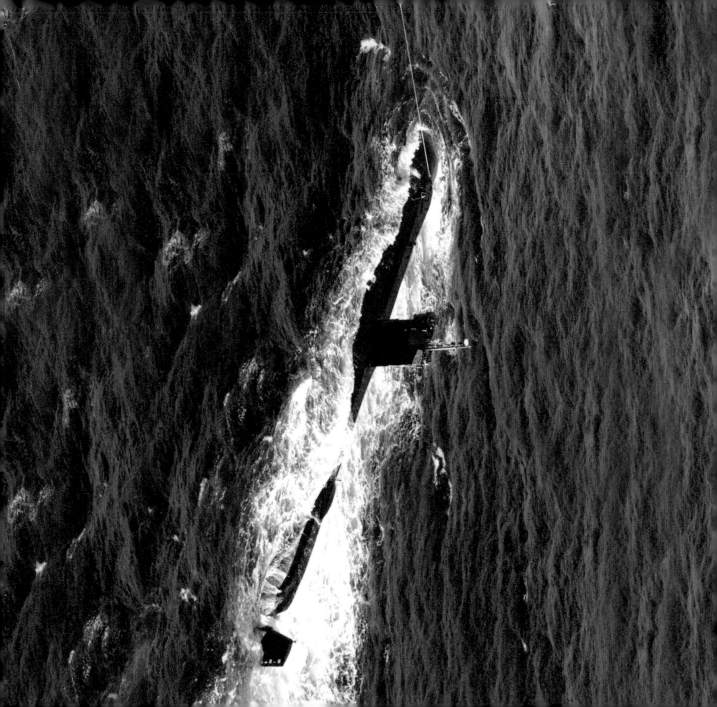

The Future of the Navy

Modern technology helps the U.S. Navy meet today's challenges. New designs will make future navy ships faster, more powerful, and better able to evade the enemy.

New ships being considered include the DD(X) destroyer, the CG(X) cruiser, and the littoral combat ship (LCS). These ships can operate in deep water or near shore. And because they share advanced technology, they are less expensive to build.

The navy is striving to be superior in technology, rather than in the size of its force. The navy of the future must respond quickly and forcefully to new threats. Ships will work closely together to use each other's strengths.

The navy strives to have the best-trained sailors and the most advanced technology available. In this way, the U.S. Navy will be ready for whatever the future holds.

The littoral combat ship (LCS) is a new type of warship. The navy hopes to use the LCS for a wide range of duties. These include surveillance, high-speed transport of sailors, and antiterrorist missions.

Glossary

aviation - the operation and navigation of aircraft. A person that operates an aircraft is called an aviator.

ballistic missile - a missile aimed before, rather than during, flight.

civil war - a war between groups in the same country. The United States of America and the Confederate States of America fought a civil war from 1861 to 1865.

civilian - of or relating to something nonmilitary.

Continental Congress - the body of representatives that spoke for and acted on behalf of the 13 colonies.

cruise missile - a guided missile that cannot fly above Earth's atmosphere.

disband - to break up something that is organized.

enlist - to join the armed forces voluntarily. An enlistee is a person who enlists for military service.

fleet - a group of ships and airplanes under one command.

Founding Fathers - the men who attended the Constitutional Convention in Philadelphia, Pennsylvania, in 1787. They helped write the U.S. Constitution.

immigration - entry into another country to live. A person who immigrates is called an immigrant.

nuclear - of or relating to the energy created when atoms are divided or combined. An atomic bomb is a nuclear weapon.

Glossary

Persian Gulf War - from January 16, 1991, to February 28, 1991. A war in the Persian Gulf to liberate Kuwait from Iraqi forces.

Revolutionary War - from 1775 to 1783. A war for independence between Great Britain and its North American colonies. The colonists won and created the United States of America.

terrorism - the use of terror, violence, or threats to frighten people into action. A person who commits an act of terrorism is called a terrorist.

War of 1812 - from 1812 to 1814. A war fought between the United States and Great Britain over shipping rights and the capture of U.S. soldiers.

World War II - from 1939 to 1945, fought in Europe, Asia, and Africa. Great Britain, France, the United States, the Soviet Union, and their allies were on one side. Germany, Italy, Japan, and their allies were on the other side.

Web Sites

To learn more about the U.S. Navy, visit ABDO Publishing Company on the World Wide Web at **www.abdopublishing.com**. Web sites about the U.S. Navy are featured on our Book Links page. These links are routinely monitored and updated to provide the most current information available.

Index

A

aircraft 4, 10, 17, 24, 25
American Civil War 10, 12, 13

B

Bonhomme Richard 12
Bureau of Ships 13

C

Congress 8, 9

D

Department of the Navy 9, 13, 14
disaster relief 4

E

Ely, Eugene 10
enemies 4, 11, 12, 22, 25, 26, 28, 29

F

Farragut, Admiral David 12, 13

H

HMS *Guerrière* 10
HMS *Serapis* 12

J

Jones, Captain John Paul 12

N

Naval Act of March 1794 9
Naval Reserve Officers' Training Corps 22, 23
Navy Reserve 16, 22

P

Persian Gulf War 22

R

Revolutionary War 8, 9, 12, 22
Rickover, Admiral Hyman G. 13

S

submarines 4, 11, 13, 26
surface ships 4, 8, 9, 10, 11, 12, 13, 16, 17, 19, 24, 25, 28, 29

U

U.S. Naval Academy 20
U.S. president 14
USS *Constitution* 10
USS *Nevada* 26
USS *Pennsylvania* 10
USS *Seawolf* 26
USS *Theodore Roosevelt* 24

W

War of 1812 10
weapons 17, 18, 24, 25, 26
World War II 11, 13, 25